21ST CENTURY DEBATES

ENDANGERED SPECIES

OUR IMPACT ON THE PLANET

MALCOLM PENNY

HODDER
Wayland

an imprint of Hodder Children's Books

21st Century Debates Series

Air Pollution • Endangered Species • Energy • Climate Change • Food Supply • Genetics •
Internet • Media • An Overcrowded World? • Rainforests • Surveillance •
Waste, Recycling and Reuse • Artificial Intelligence • Water Supply • World Health •
Global Debt • Terrorism • The Drugs Trade • Racism • Violence in Society •
Transport and the Environment • Tourism • New Religious Movements • Globalisation

Produced for Hodder Wayland by White-Thomson Publishing Ltd,
2/3 St Andrew's Place, Lewes, East Sussex BN7 1UP

© 2001 White-Thomson Publishing Ltd

Published in Great Britain in 2001 by Hodder Wayland, an imprint of Hodder Children's Books.
This paperback edition published in 2003

Project editor: Kelly Davis
Proofreader: David C. Sills, Proof Positive Reading Service
Series and book design: Christopher Halls, Mind's Eye Design, Lewes
Picture research: Shelley Noronha, Glass Onion Pictures
Internet research: Mark Baguley

British Cataloguing in Publication Data
Penny, Malcolm
   Endangered Species. - (21st century debates)
   1. Endangered species - Juvenile literature 2. Nature conservation - Juvenile literature
   I. Title
   578.6'8

ISBN 0 7502 3876 3

Printed and bound in Italy by G. Canale & C.S.p.A., Turin

Hodder Children's Books, a division of Hodder Headline Ltd, 338 Euston Road, London NW1 3BH

Picture acknowledgements: AKG 5, 6 (Jean Louis Nou), 8, 21; Bruce Coleman Collection 7 (Werner Layer), 13
(Roine Magnusson), 14 (Luiz Claudio Marigo), 17 (Jorg & Petra Wegner), 23, 28 & 58 (Gerald S. Cubitt), 21 & 57
(John Shaw), 37, 45 & 51 (Pacific Stock), 38 (Rod Williams), 47 (Geoff Dore), 48, 49 (Carol Hughes), 54; Ecoscene
42 & cover background (Wayne Lawler); Robert Harding Picture Library 32 (Duncan Maxwell); Natural History
Photographic Agency 12 (Daniel Heuclin), 20 (G.I. Bernard), 26 & cover foreground (Martin Harvey); Peter
Newark's Historical Pictures 50; Oxford Scientific 9 (Daniel Curl), 15 (Michael Leach), 16 (Adrian Bailey), 18
(Frithjob Skibbe), 24, 25, 46 (Survival Anglia), 55 (A. Huber), 56 (John McCammon); Malcolm Penny 11, 27, 36;
Popperfoto 4 (Duncan Willetts), 22, 44 (Greenpeace), 52, 59; Still Pictures 34 (Roland Seitre); Wayland Picture
Library 29, 39 (André Lichtenberg), 40; White-Thomson Publishing 33 (Steve White-Thomson); WWF 30 (Edward
Parker).

Cover: foreground picture shows a tiger in Thailand; background picture shows a subtropical rainforest.

CONTENTS

THE BIRTH OF CONSERVATION

No one is sure what a dodo looked like; it was a member of the pigeon family. This is a model made from one of the few surviving skins.

The relationship between human beings and animals is complex and ever-changing. In prehistoric times the human population was too small to be a threat to the natural world, and ancient tribal cultures evolved a way of life that had little or no impact on their environment. These traditions are still preserved by some indigenous peoples, such as those Native Americans and Australian Aborigines who try to live as their ancestors did.

In contrast, Western civilization has historically seen mankind as having 'dominion…over every living thing' (as stated in the Book of Genesis). Until relatively recently, we believed that animals existed to be farmed, hunted or exploited in any way we chose. We thought it was impossible for us to destroy a whole species. Only in the last hundred years have people begun to realize that nature is not inexhaustible.

More people, fewer animals

Ever since humans began to spread across the world, wild animals have been hunted, first for food, and later to protect mankind's great new invention, crops. About ten thousand years ago people who had previously moved about in small bands of hunter-gatherers began to form settlements where they raised livestock and grew plants to eat. For thousands of years after that, the impact of people on animals was smaller than the impact of animals on people: humans were more likely to lose their crops or their lives to a hungry animal than to threaten the survival of a species by hunting it.

But as the numbers of people grew, so did the pressure on animal populations, and not just from hunting. Some lost their natural habitat to farmers who wanted the land to grow crops, and some to people who drained wetlands (rivers, lakes and marshes) and felled forests to build villages. Today, large wild animals are scarce in the developed world, and becoming scarce even in the least developed countries. Animals now need protection from humans: too many of them have become endangered.

Alarm bells

People first realized that hunting and the destruction of habitat were causing harm to wild animal populations about a hundred and fifty years ago. Around the middle of the nineteenth century, both naturalists and Native Americans in North America noticed that some species were becoming scarce, though their warnings were mostly ignored.

VIEWPOINTS

'A cold wind blew across the prairie when the last buffalo fell ... a cold wind for my people.'
Sitting Bull, Chief of the Dakota Sioux, about 1885

'In the course of four months I killed to my own gun 42 elephants, 11 of which were big bulls, whose tusks averaged 44 lbs apiece; I also shot several very fine cows, whose tusks weighed from 15 to 16 lbs. Altogether we made a very profitable hunt.'
F.C. Selous, A Hunter's Wanderings in Africa, 1879

Sitting Bull, Chief of the Teton Dakota Indians, photographed in 1885. His Indian name was Tatanka Yotanka.

Meanwhile, in Africa, as late as 1881 'white hunters' like Frederick Courteney Selous were still plundering the bush for meat, trophies and ivory, without suspecting that the supply might one day run out.

Tiger hunting in northern India in the early eighteenth century.

In the early twentieth century, when people realized that animal numbers were falling, the white colonial rulers of African countries set up game reserves where only they and their honoured guests could enjoy hunting. In India, reserves like this were common. Their owners were the maharajahs, great local land-owners. Tigers were already scarce, because of early clearances, but survived in remaining areas of uncleared land, mostly on the big reserves. The efforts of the maharajahs and British colonial officers drove their numbers down even further, though loss of their forest habitat and loss of prey were much greater threats.

Saved for slaughter

Back in Europe, the wealthy, privileged classes had quite the opposite effect on wildlife. Here, the hunting reserves established by monarchs and nobles prevented the common people from getting their hands on game animals. They also unintentionally provided a good, safe habitat for smaller, unconsidered animals and plants, by excluding farmers and foragers.

Gran Paradiso National Park, in Italy, is a good example. It became a hunting zone in 1836, mainly for chamois; then a Royal Hunting Reserve in 1856; and a National Park in 1922. It finally received fully autonomous status in 1947. It can thus claim to be the first reserve set up to protect an individual species. However it also protects lizards and orchids that were of no interest to the hunters who originally set it up.

Preserving species, not scenery

From the eighteenth century onwards, wealthy young Britons often completed their cultural education by travelling around Europe, in what was known as the Grand Tour. They were particularly impressed by the mountainous scenery of the Alps and the Dolomites; and their descendants were delighted by the even more dramatic vistas of the American West. Yellowstone National Park in the USA was founded in 1872, to preserve the amazing geology of the region. But it was too small to provide enough food for the grizzly bears, wolves and elk that lived there. Even when the park was expanded as a sanctuary for wildlife, the wolves were shot, because they were thought to threaten the other animals. (They were reintroduced only in 1995, after much argument.)

VIEWPOINTS

'Gray wolves have made their appearance in the park in considerable numbers... Efforts will be made to kill them.'
Superintendent, Yellowstone National Park, 1914

'It is true that they may take domestic stock, and some of the sport hunter's game, but there can be no pretence that killing of wolves is justified because of danger to human lives. Wolves, like all other wildlife, have a right to exist in a wild state.'
Dr Douglas Pimlott, Chairman of the IUCN Wolf Specialist Group, 1973

Wolves have always been feared and misunderstood.

Black egret plumes were the crowning glory of a fashionable lady in 1915.

Protecting species, as opposed to scenery, began early in the twentieth century, when the Audubon Society in the USA started saving birds from the millinery trade, which had been using them to decorate ladies' hats. Gulls and egrets were the main victims. The Audubon Society began by persuading the Lighthouse Department to ban feather hunters from islands with lighthouses, using the laws against trespass. Later, Congress banned gull hunting, and wardens were appointed to guard the birds' nesting places. Today, American species-protection laws ensure that only certain animals can be hunted, and then only with the appropriate licence.

'Saving All the Parts'

By the 1980s there was growing public awareness of the clearance of temperate forests, and later the tropical rainforests, and the impact this was having on the natural world.

In 1993 Rocky Barker wrote a book called *Saving All the Parts*. Barker's book was specifically about the Pacific North-West of the United States, and how to balance the needs of the people there with the ecosystem in which they live and work. But similar problems arise elsewhere. In Australia, for example, rearing sheep threatens vast areas of grassland; and in Europe, draining wetlands puts pressure on all the species that live there.

This ecosystem approach has become the main method of conservation around the world. Although there are some animals that need to be protected as individual species, experts are agreed

VIEWPOINTS

'Wilderness has a right to exist for its own sake, and for the sake of the diversity of the life forms it shelters.'
David Foreman, Earth First, USA

'The environmentalists' demand that nature be protected against human "encroachments" means ... that man must be sacrificed in order to preserve nature. If "wilderness has a right to exist for its own sake" – then man does not.'
Peter Schwartz, Ayn Rand Institute, USA

Grazed bare and trampled flat, the outback of New South Wales is dominated and destroyed by sheep.

that the best way to conserve rare species is to protect the places where they live. This often gives rise to conflict, when businesses must sacrifice profit to protect the environment.

There are plausible arguments on both sides. Conservationists say that setting aside wildlife habitat will permit the survival of meadow plants and the insects that depend on them. Birds and small mammals will then survive in large enough numbers to feed their predators. Developers argue that the economy needs factories and housing, and intensive agriculture to feed the people. Should we let people starve, they ask, to protect orchids and barn owls?

Whose wildlife?

Although most endangered species live in developing countries, the main drive to preserve them comes from the developed world. As poorer countries develop agriculture and industry, the pressure on their wildlife increases, most often from the destruction of habitat, but sometimes from hunting for food or to protect crops.

When the animals the local people hunt are in reserves (as most of them are), the hunters are condemned as poachers. But the parks and reserves were set up in colonial times, even though they are now run by local people. So who benefits from game reserves? Who owns the endangered species? And who has the right to decide what to do with them?

To gain an understanding of these issues, we have to examine the many factors that have led to so many species becoming endangered. We can then look at different conservation strategies, and their varying degrees of success. Finally, we need to look at what lies ahead. Will it be possible to reconcile the needs of animals and humans, and create a healthy, sustainable balance in the future?

DEBATE

Should farmers be kept out of any area, at the expense of people's food, to protect an endangered species?

PEOPLE, PEOPLE EVERYWHERE

About ten thousand years ago, as we have seen, people started to grow crops and raise domestic animals. This traditional subsistence farming was successful for a very long time, but only because there were relatively few people doing it, so they had plenty of land to use. The main method of clearing land for farming then, still used in many places today, was 'slash and burn'. Conservationists oppose the use of slash-and-burn agriculture. But tropical soil scientists point out that, without advanced techniques of conserving and fertilizing the soil, it is probably better to cultivate for a short time and then leave the soil to recover.

Slash and burn is still practised every year in central Mexico, though there is not really enough land for it to work properly.

Slash and burn is a very simple way of making a vegetable patch, though it has a serious impact on the local wildlife. Every able-bodied member of the village goes to the chosen part of the forest, and cuts down everything in sight. The piles of branches and leaves are left to dry in the sun for a few days, and then burned.

When the ashes have cooled, they are ploughed into the ground, and seeds are planted. For the first year at least, the ground grows good crops. Later, sometimes even in the second year, the crops fail.

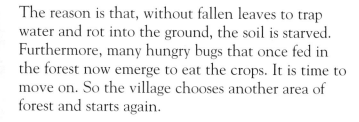

FACT

Sub-fossil remains collected in Madagascar show that there were once at least forty-five different species of lemur, ranging from animals as big as an orang-utan to some as small as a mouse. Today there are no more than twenty-eight, twelve of them highly endangered.

Southern Madagascar contains trees that are found nowhere else in the world, among them Pachypodium ('thick-foot').

The reason is that, without fallen leaves to trap water and rot into the ground, the soil is starved. Furthermore, many hungry bugs that once fed in the forest now emerge to eat the crops. It is time to move on. So the village chooses another area of forest and starts again.

The first area will recover in about four years, when it can be slashed and burned all over again. This means that a village needs five plots, each big enough to feed all its members, in order to make the system work. Slash and burn (known to them as 'milpa') supported the Maya people in Mexico for a thousand years. Some of them still use it. Finally, though, there was not enough land to feed the growing population.

A dwindling treasure

At least in Mexico the wildlife could make use of the four plots that were recovering while the villagers cultivated the fifth. The same is not true in Madagascar, where slash and burn (known there as 'tavy') has caused an ecological disaster.

The people who now live in Madagascar originally came from Indonesia, where the forest grew back every time it was left fallow. When they arrived on the huge, ancient island of Madagascar, which had been isolated for millions of years, they found a very different type of forest. It grew back only slowly, if at all, after it had been burned.

As the population grew, more and more forest was destroyed, never to recover. Torrential tropical rain washed the soil away, leaving bare, sterile hills where now nothing will grow.

The effect of this on the biodiversity of the island was catastrophic. Because of its long isolation, Madagascar supports forms of life found nowhere else on earth. Lemurs, a family of primitive primates, are the most distinctive, but the island also has birds, reptiles, insects and plants which evolved there in their own way, far from the influences that drove evolution elsewhere in the world. It is a treasure house of unique species, but many of them have become extinct, and all the rest are endangered, because of the impact of tavy agriculture.

VIEWPOINT

'...looking down at the maimed earth, one is brought almost to tears by the tragedy of Madagascar's most significant statistic – three-quarters of the island's surface is officially classified as "severely degraded".'
Dervla Murphy, Muddling Through in Madagascar, *1985*

The sifaka ('sheefark') is one of the largest surviving lemurs, now carefully protected in a few small reserves. Its name comes from its call.

FACT

The Yanomami people are a tribe of hunter-gatherers in the forests of Brazil. During an outbreak of malaria in 1998, they showed scientists eighty-two different plants that they use to treat the disease. All were found to contain chemicals effective against malaria.

The gentle life

In the rainforests, there are still tribes of hunter-gatherers who live as their distant ancestors did, in harmony with their surroundings. They hunt in the forest, fish in the rivers, and find fruits and seeds among the trees, leaving scarcely a trace of their passing. They are creatures of the forest just as much as the jaguars and hummingbirds that are their neighbours. But one reason why these gentle people have not overwhelmed their environment with a population explosion might well be that their life is hard, and often brief, and many of their children do not survive into adulthood.

The Yanomami Indians find all they need in the forest. Here, a palm-fibre basket is given a waterproof covering of banana leaves.

In other parts of the world, there are forms of simple agriculture that have very little impact on the environment. On the open plains of Mongolia, or the tundra of Lapland, nomadic pastoralists tend their herds of cattle or reindeer without noticeable effects on their surroundings. They hunt for food as they move from one pasture to another with the seasons.

A barn owl and her chicks find warmth and comfort on a bale of hay.

A man-made landscape

These ancient forms of agriculture developed slowly, which meant that any wildlife affected by human activity was able to adapt to it. Even in Europe, where early agriculture had a much more marked effect on the landscape and the environment, many animals adapted well to living in farmland.

Meadow-nesting birds like skylarks, and forest-edge species like blackbirds, probably multiplied dramatically when the old forests were cleared over a thousand years ago. The hedge sparrow, now called a dunnock, even takes its old English name (and its present German, Dutch and Swedish names) from the hedge, an agricultural feature originally introduced about eight hundred years ago to protect livestock from wolves. The barn owl and the North American barn swallow are also named after the farm building where they most often nest.

The small arable fields and open pastures of European farmland became valuable habitats in their own right. And everything continued peacefully for a thousand years – until the human population began to increase, and people and animals had to compete for living space. The endangering of species had begun.

VIEWPOINT

'The countryside must not be frozen in time, but the decline in wildlife and habitats must be reversed.'
Michael Meacher, British Environment Minister.

DEBATE

Are people just another animal species, entitled to compete with other animals in taking what they need from the earth?

SELF-DEFENCE

FACT

During the building of the Uganda railway in 1898, two lions killed twenty-eight Indian construction workers and dozens of Africans. When they were finally hunted down and shot, they were found to be perfectly normal males.

Some animals are a threat to people, either as predators or because they have harmful ways of defending themselves, like being poisonous. The human response has always been the same: we try to kill them. As a result, many of them have become endangered. Mountain lions and rattlesnakes in the Americas, wolves and adders in Europe, tigers and cobras in India, lions and puff adders in Africa – the list stretches round the world. Protecting these unpopular animals is not easy, especially when they eat people.

Man-eaters

It is often said that a healthy lion will not attack humans – as if man-eating were the last resort of old, sick lions. But there are plenty of reports of perfectly fit lions eating people. Man-eating is rare enough to get into the world's newspapers when it happens, but common enough to make it hard to argue in defence of lions when African people want to reduce their numbers.

Tigers, too, eat people. For the Indian maharajahs, killing a tiger was regarded as an admirable, almost heroic act, not least because it was seen as a service to the local villagers. One maharajah boasted that he had killed 1,500 tigers in his lifetime.

A young, healthy lioness in the Okavango Delta, Botswana.

Later, it became something for Europeans to brag about in their clubs, in rooms liberally carpeted with tiger skins. Sportsmen from all over the world went to India to hunt tigers.

These attitudes seem barbaric today, when the tiger is one of the main examples of animals needing protection from human killers, but tigers are still a real danger in rural India. Even now, when they are rare and mostly confined to carefully guarded reserves, tigers still emerge from the forest to attack people working in the fields.

Fears and phobias

Sometimes the fear that drives people to kill animals is groundless. Arachnophobia, for example, is a real threat to spiders all over the world. Although some spiders are very poisonous (like the redback and the brown recluse in Australia), most are harmless. All the same, many people are terrified of them and will kill them on sight.

VIEWPOINTS

'The shock ... caused a sort of dreaminess, in which there was no sense of pain nor feeling of terror... This peculiar state is probably produced in all animals killed by the carnivora ... a merciful provision by our benevolent Creator...'
David Livingstone, the famous African explorer, on being attacked by a lion in 1844

'Several Kafirs who have been bitten [by lions] have told me ... that they felt the most acute anguish: I can only conclude that this especial mercy is one which Providence does not extend beyond ministers of the Gospel.'
F.C. Selous, 1879, having read Livingstone's description

Bird-eating spiders are harmless to people, but not many would try this!

FACT

The Tasmanian 'tiger' was hunted to extinction on Tasmania by Europeans. A large marsupial carnivore, it probably became extinct on the Australian mainland as a result of the spread of the dingo (wild dog) which the first human settlers brought with them from New Guinea about 7,000 years ago.

VIEWPOINTS

'...when nature is thought of as evil, you don't put yourself in accord with it, you control it, or try to, and hence ... the cutting down of forests...'
Joseph Campbell, The Power of Myth, 1988

'We [environmentalists] are not interested in the utility of a particular species ... or ecosystem to mankind. They have intrinsic value, more value – to me – than another human body, or a billion of them...'
David Graber, a biologist with the US National Park Service

Other phobias threaten other types of animal. Almost all primates, including humans, have an instinctive fear of snakes. Other primates will avoid them, but humans have the means and the determination to kill any snake they see. Many African people fear chameleons in the same way; and in Madagascar people used to kill aye-ayes (one of the rarest lemurs) whenever they saw them. Elsewhere people kill owls because they think of them as omens of death. These superstitious reasons for killing are the hardest to fight against in the battle to preserve endangered species.

Fear of the forest

Irrational fears can harm animals indirectly, too, when their habitat is destroyed because people think of it as hostile. Many fairytales depict the wild wood as a frightening place, infested with hungry wolves, and the lonely marsh as haunted by weird spirits. As soon as they could, people felled the forests and drained the marshes, not only to use the land for farming and living space, but also to make them feel safe. The animals that lived there were the losers.

Regarded as haunted and dangerous, marshes were feared by our ancestors.

SHOOTING FOR FUN AND PROFIT

People hunt and kill animals for reasons other than self-defence. On some Mediterranean islands they regularly slaughter small migratory birds. In Cyprus the local people call them *ambelopoulia* ('vine birds'), and the hunt takes place twice a year.

Once its purpose was to protect the flowering grape vines in spring, and the fruit in autumn. But now it has turned into a ritual, in which as many as 5,000 hunters go out on the first day of the autumn season. Their aim is no longer to protect the vines, but to kill as many birds as they can. They shoot migrating warblers, flycatchers and thrushes – anything within range of their increasingly powerful guns. The dead birds are either barbecued and eaten at once, or pickled and bottled, often for export to their friends in other countries, including England, where there is a large Cypriot community.

Since the birds are migrants, travelling between their breeding grounds in northern Europe and their wintering grounds in Africa, the hunt in Cyprus affects the bird population over a wide area beyond the island.

A similar hunt takes place on Malta, where some of the birds are stuffed for collections, in much the same way as Victorian naturalists collected butterflies. In southern Italy, hunters shoot migrating birds of prey, most of them protected by law in all the countries on their route.

VIEWPOINT

'The first day sees about 5,000 hunters out, heavily camouflaged and looking faintly ridiculous. Indeed I often think that the best way of combating the Mediterranean hunting phenomenon would be ... to get over to them just how ridiculous they do look.'
Peter Cant, Honorary Secretary, North Cyprus Society for the Protection of Birds, 1991, letter to the author

Estimated numbers of some migrant birds killed each year by bird collectors on Malta

Species	No. shot each year	No. stuffed each year
Marsh Harrier	9,700	6,400
Honey Buzzard	3,200	3,500
Cuckoo	55,000	5,100
Nightjar	32,000	1,600
Swift	100,000+	none
Robin	100,000+	none
Thrushes	300,000+	8,400
Golden Oriole	80,000	7,800
Finches	1-2 million	none

From Fatal Flight *by Natalino Fenech, published by Quiller Press, 1992*

Activities like these make it easier to understand how the passenger pigeon came to be shot to extinction – simply because it was so common, and such an easy target.

FACT

The passenger pigeon, which migrated over North America, was wiped out by shooting. Before 1840, there were between five and nine billion birds. Too late, a few survivors were protected. The last of them, a female, died in Cincinnati Zoo on 1 September 1914.

A passenger pigeon, drawn from life in 1850, when they were still common.

The fall and rise of the buffalo

The destruction of the huge population of buffalo in North America is a well-known story – but recent research has put a twist in the tale. In 1800, there were probably about sixty million buffalo on the Great Plains. In the 1880s, professional European hunters moved in, killing hundreds of thousands a year. They shot them mainly for their skins, which were valuable in the cities for rugs and coats, and for meat. Some were killed only for their tongues, which were cut out in the field, leaving the remains for the wolves – which flourished at the time. By 1885, about thirty million buffalo had been killed, and the species was practically extinct.

Even when they had horses, the Plains Indians needed great skill and courage to hunt buffalo. This coloured woodcut, based on a painting by George Catlin, was published in 1848.

But the destruction of the buffalo had begun nearly a century earlier, at the hands of the Plains Indians. The Lakota Sioux first acquired horses in about 1720, from herds wandering north from Mexico, where the Spaniards had introduced them a couple of hundred years before. Horses revolutionized their hunting technique: previously, they had had to stalk buffalo on foot and kill them with spears, a dangerous business. Now they could kill as many as they pleased. Sometimes they would use the horses to round up the buffalo and drive a whole herd over a cliff to die. They would then take the meat they wanted, leaving hundreds of carcasses to rot.

By 1850, they had slaughtered half of the sixty million, some of them to make robes to sell to European settlers advancing across the Plains, and

DEBATE

Is hunting for sport a legitimate pastime? What about hunting for food? What regulations might be necessary to preserve the quarry species?

the rest for meat. Realizing that the slaughter had got out of hand, they began to take steps to reduce the numbers killed – but then the white hunters arrived, to finish the job the Indians had started.

Buffalo hides shipped east from the prairies

Year	No. of hides shipped
1881	50,000
1882	200,000
1883	40,000
1884	300

From The Buffalo Book, *by David A. Dary, 1974*

In the later stages of the hunt, the authorities could see exactly what would happen, but they allowed and even encouraged the slaughter. Denying the Indians the buffalo on which their lives depended was a way of bringing them too to the edge of extinction. When Europeans arrived on the Great Plains there were about seven million Indians: by 1900 there were just 250,000 left. But the story was not finished yet. The Indians were never to recover their old way of life, but the buffalo would return.

A Sioux Indian camp in the nineteenth century, when buffalo were becoming scarce. The chief's sword and tunic may be battle trophies.

SPECIES CONSERVATION

Even while the buffalo was being wiped out, efforts to save it had begun. Several ranchers had small herds on their properties as early as 1866, originally as a hobby, but increasingly with the intention of raising and killing them like cattle.

As National Parks began to be established, buffalo from these private herds were moved into them. The herd in Yellowstone National Park was started in 1902, with eighteen animals from two private herds. A herd of 700 was moved to Elk Island Park, in Alberta, Canada, in 1912. Within twenty years of its destruction as a wild animal of the plains, the buffalo became an emblem of the growing movement to save animal species from extinction at the hands of humanity. Many other species were to follow.

More recently, there has been a strange development in the story of the buffalo. In 1990 a buffalo conservation programme was set up on a Sioux reservation in South Dakota. By 2000 the herd numbered 1,500 animals. Then, to the dismay of conservationists, the Sioux people bought a mobile slaughterhouse, and started to butcher the buffalo for sale. However, the Sioux pointed out that they were only following their ancient tradition, in making use of the animal that they have always revered.

Buffalo in Yellowstone National Park. Before 1850, they would have covered the hills.

FACT

In Chinese traditional medicine tiger tail bones are ground up and used to treat skin complaints, the whiskers are used as a protective charm, the brain is made into an ointment to cure acne, and the penis is believed to act as an aphrodisiac (strengthening sexual desire).

Project Tiger

Early conservation operations were aimed at preserving individual species when they were shown to be in imminent danger of extinction. The first in recent times was intended to save the tiger.

Pressure on the tiger in India had become so great that in 1972 there were found to be only 1,800 individuals, from a population in 1930 of at least 40,000. The causes were loss of habitat, over-hunting, and a brisk and very lucrative trade, not only in skins but also in parts of tigers, to be used in Chinese traditional medicine. Project Tiger was organized by the World Wildlife Fund (WWF, now – with the same initials – called the World Wide Fund for Nature).

Every National Park in India took part in Project Tiger. Sariska is in the north of the country.

The main aim of the Project was to persuade the Indian government to ban tiger hunting, while setting up tiger reserves in the best habitat areas. The results were dramatic: over the next fourteen years, the tiger population in the whole of India more than doubled, to an estimated 4,000 in 1989. As the years went by, some reserves reported better results than others. For example, in the Sundarbans (an area of mangrove islands on the border between north-eastern India and Bangladesh) the population rose from 242 tigers in 1995 to 262 in 1997, including twenty-five new cubs. But there has been a downside to this success story.

Hungry for tigers

The demand for tiger products for tourists and for medicinal use in the Far East has risen steadily.

Tigers are even sometimes caught and killed for meat, especially by Chinese poachers along the Burmese border. The meat sells for about $50 per pound. Now that there are more tigers in India, and the poachers know where they are, the killing goes on.

FACT

Tiger teeth, worn as a good luck pendant, are sold to tourists for as much as $300 each, claws for $150, and skins for $1,000 or more.

Poached skins of tigers and leopards are confiscated to stop them being sold – but the killing goes on because the rewards are so high.

VIEWPOINTS

'WWF remains absolutely resolute in its determination to fight the battle to save the tiger – we have done it once before in the early 1970s, and now we must do it again.'
Robin Pellew, Director, WWF-UK, 1999

'Many people are unwilling to face the fact that tigers have very specific needs. In Nagarahole, among a population of 20 pairs of breeding tigers, each female needs 15 sq km. That's a total of ... 300-400 sq km.'
Dr Ullas Karanth, Wildlife Conservation Society, USA

Facts are hard to come by, because the trade is illegal and therefore undercover, but it was legal in South Korea until 1993. Records there show that between 1975 and 1992 they imported more than 6 tonnes of tiger bones (representing more than 550 and possibly 1,000 tigers). The average was 577 kg per year (or about 50–100 tigers). Until 1991, the main supplier was Indonesia, replaced by China for the last two years on record, but where the tigers were killed was not clear.

Furthermore, the rate at which tiger habitat outside the reserves is being destroyed for farmland has been increasing. In 1999 the WWF launched a new initiative to save all surviving tiger species, spending half a million dollars in the first half of the year. The results remain to be seen.

FACT

In the People's Republic of China, more than 10,000 bears are kept on bear farms so that they can be 'milked' of their bile through tubes inserted into their gall bladders. In South Korea, bear bile is used to treat serious liver diseases such as cirrhosis or cancer. The price to the patient in 1993 was about $40 per gram.

The Bengal tiger of India and Nepal is the best-known species, but tigers live in a number of other countries. South-east Asia, from Myanmar (Burma) to Vietnam, is the home of the Indo-Chinese tiger, of which perhaps 1,800 survive. In Indonesia, where the Bali and Javan tigers have become extinct, there may be more than 500 Sumatran tigers still alive. Laos, Malaysia, Thailand and China all have remnant tiger populations. In the far east of Russia, the Siberian or Amur tiger survived heavy poaching in the early 1990s, and as many as 500 are to be protected by a new system of reserves.

Not just tigers

Setting up reserves to protect the habitat of the tiger benefited many other species, including elephants and rhinos, bison and deer, and also the rare golden langur, a long-tailed monkey with a very restricted range. This came as no surprise to the organizers, but it suggested a broader approach to the conservation of other species.

In addition to this, the new reserves attracted growing numbers of tourists, who brought substantial amounts of foreign currency into the national park system, and into India as a whole. This will turn out to be an important thread in the conservation story.

The tiger has become a symbol of conservation – but saving the tiger will save many other animals as well.

POACHING AND TRADE

One reason for the endangered status of many large wild animals today is poaching, which means illegal hunting. As we have seen in the case of the tiger, this may be done for food, or to provide souvenirs for tourists, or – more often – to supply the market for medicinal products in the Far East.

Not only the tiger but also all five species of rhino are endangered by poaching, mainly for medicinal purposes. The world's eight species of bears are killed for parts of their bodies to be used as medicine. Elephants are poached for their ivory, as well as for elephant hair bracelets and containers made from their feet. Even gorillas are killed to provide souvenirs – though bushmeat hunting is probably more of a threat to them today.

The debate about poaching is complex, because it concerns ownership. No-one can actually own a wild animal: by definition, a wild animal is one that is not under human control. However, animals protected by law may be said to belong to the state, and the government of that state therefore has a right to stop them being stolen.

Orphaned guenons being hand-reared in Nigeria. Their mother was killed for bushmeat. Many rare primates, including drills, guenons and mangabeys, are becoming endangered because of this trade.

These white rhino horns were recovered in Kruger National Park, South Africa.

FACT

Between July 1984 and early June 1988, guards on Zimbabwe's northern border shot and killed thirty-nine rhino poachers, and sent at least thirty others to prison.

VIEWPOINTS

'...every hour of every day poachers kill one more elephant for its bloody ivory'
Born Free Foundation, UK

'...although legal ivory trade involves the death of a particular elephant, it may be the surest way to protect the species.'
Roger Bate, Fellow of the Institute of Economic Affairs, UK

DEBATE

Should people be shot for trying to poach endangered animals?

Local politicians often argue that national parks are no different from the game reserves set up in colonial times, that the native people own the animals, and should not be prevented from using them as they always have. This implies that they want to kill them for food or to protect their crops, but the most common reason for poaching today is for trade.

The incentive for the poacher is that the prices offered for rhino horn, ivory, or bear parts, for example, are enormous by the standards of rural people. A Chinese poacher who kills a tiger on the Burmese border can earn more than a year's wages for doing it. In the 1980s a gang that went from Zambia to Zimbabwe to hunt for black rhinos would have been rich men if they could have got the horns home again. Many of them did not return, however, being shot by armed guards as they landed. Black rhino poaching has now almost stopped in Zimbabwe, since all the surviving rhinos are held in guarded enclosures. But there are some animals that are impossible to guard or enclose.

PROTECTING SPECIES

Although elephants are under severe pressure from ivory poaching in many parts of Africa, in some places their numbers are actually too high. In Zimbabwe's Hwange National Park, for example, the population of about 2,000 elephants is growing faster than the park can support. They produce 200 young a year, and there is nowhere for them to go.

The park is surrounded by farmland. Local farmers torment elephants that break out of the park until they move on, or sometimes kill them. Inside the fence there is not enough food for them. In trying to find food, they destroy the park's vegetation, and the habitat of all the other animals that live there – not to mention the park's appeal to tourists (its main source of income). In the 1980s, when the problem first became severe, some way had to be found of limiting elephant numbers.

Young elephants need constant care and guidance when they have no family to bring them up.

On the move

At first, relocation seemed to be the answer, moving the elephants to other parts of Africa where they had become rare, or even to zoos; but this raised more problems than it solved.

Elephants are large and awkward to move, to say the least. Furthermore, they are family animals: it was soon realized that removing young animals from the influence of

their mother and aunts produces mental and behavioural difficulties in later life. It is necessary to move whole families together – which is plainly an enormous undertaking.

Sentence of death

Finally, and very reluctantly, the management of Hwange National Park decided that culling – a polite word for killing – the elephants was the only answer. This, like relocation, has to be done to whole families. Shooting some members and letting the others go free produces a group of severely traumatized elephants, bereaved and demented, who will cause trouble for the rest of their lives. The resulting scenes were horrific to outsiders – and the world's press was quick to publish photographs of elephant herds being rounded up with helicopters and massacred by men with rifles.

Nevertheless the cull went ahead. The elephants were skinned, and the meat distributed to local people. The tusks were removed, as well as the wiry hairs from their tails (used to make bracelets worn by men and women all over Africa). But, because of international animal conservation regulations, none of these valuable products could be sold, even though the revenue from them would have financed the park into the distant future.

Jawbones of poached elephants collected in Namibia in the 1980s, when hundreds were killed by Angolan poachers.

Everything was stored in a huge warehouse at Hwange until the hoped-for day when the regulations might be changed. This finally happened in 1999, when ivory from elephants from Botswana, Namibia and Zimbabwe was allowed to be sold to Japan, but only from existing government stocks, and only one shipment.

The rhino's dilemma

The pressure on four of the world's five species of rhino is even greater than that on the tiger or the elephant. Not only are they much sought-after for medicinal parts, used all over the world wherever there is a Chinese community, but until very recently they were persecuted for their horns, to make the handles of *jambias*, the ceremonial daggers worn by young men in the Yemen when they reach adulthood. There are signs that this fashion has changed, and other less expensive materials – such as gold – are now more acceptable, but the demand for medicines goes on.

Black rhinos can be aggressive when cornered or surprised, but they have no defence against high-powered rifles.

Alpine ibex in Gran Paradiso National Park, Italy, rescued from extinction.

FACT

The Alpine ibex was hunted to the brink of extinction in the nineteenth century to collect horns and gall bladders for use in European medicines. It was rescued by captive breeding, reintroduction and careful management; but we should not be too scornful of those who kill rhinos to make medicines.

Pills and potions

Almost every part of a rhino is used as a cure, in various different schools of medicine. It is not true, though it is widely believed in the West, that the horn is used exclusively as an aphrodisiac: instead, it is used to cure conditions ranging from piles to arthritis, including fevers and even polio. The skin is a good luck charm, keeping diseases away, and the blood, faeces and urine all have their uses. Fat and strips of stomach are also regarded as valuable treatments, for polio and skin diseases respectively.

Although the use of rhino products has decreased in Myanmar (Burma), this is because that country has become very poor in the last few decades, so that people can no longer afford expensive medicines. In wealthier eastern countries, such as Japan and Korea, the rising standard of living has coincided with a return to the traditional medicine introduced from China more than a thousand years ago. Far from falling, the demand for rhino products is rising in those countries.

Given that rhino horn sells for $25,000 per kilo in Kuala Lumpur, for example, and even dried skin can cost nearly $500, the middleman can offer the poacher enormous sums of money. For this reason the poacher feels it is worth risking his life trying to kill a rhino.

Substitutes

The way to protect the remaining rhinos from poaching would seem to be to convince eastern doctors and pharmacists that there are good substitutes for rhino products in the treatment of disease. Experiments using the ground-up horn of saiga antelope from Russia, an easily available by-product of a commercial harvest, have so far proved inconclusive. The best hope might be that as rhino products become more expensive and harder to get, eastern medical practitioners will become more convinced of the success of western 'scientific' medicine. The salvation of the rhino might well lie in medical schools rather than in new laws – or more guns and rangers – to protect it.

FACT

Since 1970, the number of black rhinos in all of Africa has fallen from 65,000 to about 2,700. Careful protection against poaching, and better understanding of how they use their habitat has stabilized their numbers, though the species is still in great danger.

Cape buffalo are regarded by hunters as the fiercest animal in Africa. Their powdered horn was once used in traditional medicine.

The Sumatran rhino was widely distributed until the end of the nineteenth century, through Thailand and into Bengal and Assam. Today, it survives only in the southern part of its former range.

Meanwhile, the battle to save the rhino goes on. The only species that is safe is the southern white rhino, in its various sanctuaries in South Africa. The African black rhino has a good, well-defended population in South Africa too, as well as in Zimbabwe and Botswana, though it is under desperate pressure elsewhere in Africa. The one-horned Indian/Nepalese rhino is relatively safe in half a dozen reserves, the Sumatran rhino hangs on

Species	Location	No. in 2000
Black rhino	Africa	2,700
White rhino	Africa	10,400
One-horned rhino	India, Nepal	2,400
Javan rhino	Indonesia, Vietnam	60
Sumatran rhino	Borneo, Malaya, Sumatra	300
	Total in Africa:	13,100
	Total in Asia:	2,760

in three countries, and the Javan rhino exists only in one reserve, Ujong Kulong, in Java, and some have recently been discovered in Vietnam.

Saving African rhinos: the great white hope

The white rhino has two separate races: one in the north that lives only in Zaire, where twenty-five individuals survived in 1999 (there were 821 of them in 1980, half in Sudan and half in Zaire); and a southern race whose story is completely different, and offers hope for other endangered animals.

It was thought to be extinct in 1892, but a small group of white rhino was found in 1897, in the valley of the Umfolozi river in Natal. The government declared the valley a reserve, and the population increased until there were thirty rhino in 1930, and 1,500 in 1960. During that time, 500 rhino had been shipped out to other parks, and to zoos around the world. The white rhino population of South Africa is now at full capacity – which can lead to another moral dilemma, as we have seen.

In the black corner...

The black rhino has been fighting a losing battle for many years, though with many allies among humans. In countries north of the Zambezi river it is virtually extinct, but it has a secure population in South Africa and a staunchly defended foothold in Zimbabwe, where private landowners have clubbed together to form a rhino reserve. There is another in Kenya, also financed by private donations. Research by Ron Thomson, the pioneering wildlife biologist, has shown that animals like rhinos breed fastest if they are kept at half the carrying capacity of the area where they live. Using this technique has enabled these protected populations to multiply at a very satisfactory rate.

FACT

A group of white rhinos were transported by sea and road to Whipsnade Zoo in England in the 1960s, from the rapidly expanding population in Umfolozi. Nearly forty years later, all the original animals have died, but their descendants still live in a large reserve in the zoo.

VIEWPOINT

'While it may seem gruesome to some, there is no doubt that trophy hunting provides huge incentives to protect wildlife throughout Africa.'
Michael De Alessi, Institute of Economic Affairs

FACT

One white oryx herd
lives in the Arava
Valley, in southern
Israel, and another
over the border in
Jordan. In 1995, during
a truce between the
two countries, it was
decided to open the
border and let the
herds interbreed, to
widen their gene pool.
However, the truce
broke down, and the
two herds are still
separate, both in
danger from inbreeding.

Saving the oryx

Another success story about saving an individual species concerns the Arabian (or white) oryx, a graceful desert antelope that was once extinct in the wild. It had been hunted for centuries by Bedouin tribesmen in its desert home, on foot or from camel-back with primitive rifles, without serious harm. But when they acquired modern rifles and jeeps after the Second World War, they shot it almost to extinction by 1972. Its rescue began in 1962, when the Fauna Preservation Society (now called Flora and Fauna International), seeing trouble ahead, organized Operation Oryx.

They established a world herd of captive oryx in Phoenix, Arizona, where the animals were carefully bred in preparation for the day when ecological – and especially social – conditions in central Oman were safe for its return. This happened in 1982, and the species is once more safe in the wild. There are two other herds, in Jordan and Israel. Captive breeding of this kind is often thought to be a last resort, but it has saved more than one species from almost certain extinction.

White oryx in the breeding reserve at Yotvata, southern Israel. In the background are onagers (wild asses) that have also been sucessfully released into the wild.

CAPTIVE BREEDING

Some species become so rare that the only way to keep them alive is to try to breed them in captivity. The first example was the Hawaiian goose, often called by its local name, the nene (pronounced 'neh-nay'). In its island home it was in danger of being wiped out by cats and other introduced domestic animals that had become feral (gone wild).

A pair of nene, back home in Hawaii in a sanctuary cleared of their many enemies.

From an estimated population of 25,000 in the eighteenth century, its numbers had fallen to no more than thirty by 1951. In 1945, the biologist P.H. Baldwin made a formidable list of the nene's problems on Hawaii.

Activities of man:
Exploration
Hunting with firearms
Probable increase in capture of live birds and eggs
Flushing and frightening birds from nests and
    foraging grounds
Sandalwood gathering in uplands
Ranching developments and activities
Building of beach resort homes and of military
    roads in uplands
Indirect results of the white man's activities:
Introduced animals such as the rat, goat, sheep,
    cow, horse, pig (European), ass, feral dog and
    cat, mongoose, gamebirds (pheasant, quail,
    guinea hen, jungle fowl, turkey, peafowl),
    the mynah, and the ant
Introduced plants such as pasture weeds, mesquite,
    thimble-berry, and pampas grass

Poison arrow frogs produce a deadly toxin from their skin. In spite – or perhaps because – of this, they are much sought-after by collectors in Europe.

FACT

Poison arrow frogs from Central America used to be seriously threatened by the trade in live specimens captured from the forest. But when frogs confiscated from smugglers were given to expert frog-breeders in Britain they managed to produce such large numbers that the price plummeted. This meant that the trade was no longer worthwhile for the poachers and smugglers.

Looking at this list, it seemed as though the goose had no chance of survival in the wild on the island. The only hope of saving it was to take it prisoner. Two breeding centres were set up, one at Pohakuloa on Hawaii in 1949, and the other at Slimbridge, England, in 1951. After many setbacks and problems, both managed to breed healthy flocks of nenes, from which birds were released back into the wild, beginning in 1963.

By the end of the project, 1,500 captive-bred birds had been released. Their main home on the island is in sanctuaries from which as many as possible of their enemies have been removed. The survival of the species is guaranteed, not only by the released birds living on Hawaii, but by hundreds of captive pairs held by wildfowl collectors all over the world.

A captive deer

Another one of the very few species saved from extinction by captive breeding is Père David's deer, from China, which has been known in historical times only from parks and zoos. However, there are serious problems involved in keeping small captive populations, the main one being a lack of genetic diversity, leading to inbreeding and loss of fertility. Without natural predators and diseases to weed out the weaker young animals, the species might change from its original form into one that would be unable to survive in the wild.

Tampering with nature

Human interference with the ecosystem often puts it off balance. When predators are reduced or eliminated, perhaps to protect domestic stock, their prey animals often increase to a level where they become a nuisance. This happens in parts of the US, where wolves, mountain lions and grizzly bears have become rare because of persecution. Consequently, deer become too numerous, and have to be shot to control their numbers. In New Zealand, where deer were introduced by European settlers, they began to destroy the native forests, and must still be culled regularly, sometimes by shooting from helicopters.

FACT

Parrots are also a captive breeding success story. Large macaws from the Amazon forest and African Grey parrots from the Congo can fetch thousands of dollars. But, like poison arrow frogs, parrots breed readily in captivity, and there is no longer any need to capture them in the wild.

Scarlet macaws are still poached in Brazil, but captive breeding is helping to supply the demand without any more being taken from the Amazon forests.

FACT

One problem in breeding giant pandas in captivity is that they are so valuable that zoos are reluctant to send them to where they might have a better chance of success. Another is that pandas become so accustomed to humans that they do not recognize another panda as a potential mate.

The reluctant panda

The giant panda has become the symbol of species protection, not least because it was chosen as the emblem of the World Wide Fund for Nature (WWF). Only about 1,000 pandas survive in the wild, most of them in carefully guarded reserves, the biggest of which is at Wolong, in China's Sichuan Province. Much-publicized attempts at breeding them in zoos have met with little success. Many different drugs have been tried – even including Viagra, allegedly – and panda pairs have been shown films of other pandas mating, to no avail.

However, in September 2000, Wolong had a panda baby boom, when six cubs were born in four days to pandas in the breeding centre on the reserve. In the midst of the triumphant announcements, the Chinese government media reported that the population boom was the result of a 37-year campaign to improve the pandas' habitat by replacing farmland with forest, so as to improve the air and water quality in the area. The pandas' main problem had been their loss of available habitat to encroaching agriculture. This habitat approach to conservation has long been seen as the best hope for protecting endangered species.

The giant panda is perhaps the best-loved animal in the world, though very rarely seen in the wild.

SAVING HABITATS

Many of the world's rarest species, especially birds, live on islands. The Seychelles paradise flycatcher, the Bermuda petrel, the Mauritius kestrel: the list seems to consist almost entirely of the name of an island followed by the name of a bird. Other rarities are reptiles, including the tuatara, said to be the only surviving dinosaur, which lives on the smallest islands of New Zealand, the giant tortoises of the Galapagos, and the Komodo dragon, a huge predatory lizard – which bears the name of the island which is its last home. This is not a coincidence.

Animals that live on islands are especially vulnerable to invaders from outside. They have evolved to live with minimal competition from their neighbours, so that when newcomers arrive – usually brought in by people – the residents often have no defence. Introduced species, both domestic animals (like those that threatened the Hawaiian goose) and accidental imports (such as rats and sparrows), are able to out-compete and out-breed the residents. Baldwin's list of the problems facing the nene applies in general terms to all the islands in the world.

Islands old and new

As the world's wild places become smaller and fewer, many of them effectively become 'islands', isolated patches of wilderness in a sea of humanity. But Jonathan Kingdon's book *Island Africa*, published in 1989, argues that this is not a new, man-made phenomenon. Lakes, isolated forests in seas of grassland, and mountains rearing up from

FACT

Hawksbill turtles, the source of tortoiseshell, used to make jewellery and ornaments, are now protected from hunting in the Seychelles, one of their main breeding areas in the Indian Ocean.

FACT

The sixteen Galápagos islands are home to many unique animal species, and 40 per cent of Galápagos' vegetation is found nowhere else in the world.

FACT

In some countries, such as the Philippines, there is almost no rainforest left. In others, fragments remain which could be preserved. Paraguay was half covered in forest in 1940; by 1990 only a third of the country was forested.

level plains were all natural landlocked islands long before humans came on the scene. Learning to understand places like this is vitally important in order to conserve the world's wildlife.

Today, habitat protection is the main aim of conservation. It is not easy to balance the needs of humans with those of wild animals and non-commercial plants, but it is essential if any of the wild world is to survive. However, this can give rise to complex moral and social problems.

A mountain stream trickles through rainforest in northern Australia. Could this be the richest and most diverse habitat on earth?

The dwindling rainforests

The felling of the tropical rainforests started long ago, when bands of hunter-gatherers began to settle in semi-permanent villages where they could grow crops. For thousands of years, as we have seen, they did little or no harm to the environment.

This is because, when forest people clear small areas with hand tools, they usually leave large trees standing, because they are hard to fell. These trees provide seeds from which the forest can grow back. The people also leave dead trees alone, because they are too big or too dangerous to move. Rotting, fallen trees and dead tree stumps provide homes for a huge variety of animals and plants. But commercial logging companies use heavy machinery to clear the land completely.

When they have finished, there are no seeds for the future, and no homes for other creatures. Land that has been clear-cut is often used for cattle ranching. When the cattle have eaten all the grass and trampled the soft forest soil, it becomes a worthless wasteland. Also, the roads made by the loggers allow more people into the forest, so that poaching becomes more common.

Whose forests?

Most European forests were cleared for farmland in the Middle Ages, and in India they were cut and burned for firewood even earlier. There is now evidence that the North American prairies were created and maintained by regular burning by the Native Americans over thousands of years. This makes the remaining rainforests even more valuable, but the question is: valuable to whom?

The people who live in them today, if they carry on in the old way, can live by hunting, fishing, and growing crops in clearings, just as they have

FACT

Scientists say that 10 per cent of the Amazon rainforest has now been cleared (about 100 sq km). Meanwhile, in the Pacific North-West of the USA, 87 per cent of the temperate rainforests has been cleared.

FACT

Coral reefs are communities of animal colonies, formed by tiny relatives of sea anemones. They catch some food from the water, but the rest comes from small photosynthetic cells that live inside them. Thus they need clear water to let the sunlight through, but some debris to eat.

With countless species of fish and invertebrates, coral reefs rival rainforests as the most productive of earth's habitats.

throughout history. But who are we to insist that they continue their Stone Age existence in a world of computers and sophisticated healthcare? Their forest home is worth a lot of money, when the trees are felled and sold as timber. They could use the money to bring themselves into the twenty-first century. It often seems to be other people who want the rainforests to survive, ecologists and conservationists who live in distant cities.

Most older tribal people (and some young ones) want to preserve their traditional way of life, while most young people (and some older ones) want the material advantages of modern technology. In Irian Jaya, in New Guinea, for example, the people live in traditional villages but use modern communications such as TV and two-way radio.

Killing reefs

Some people say that the tropical rainforests are the greatest example of biodiversity on earth, while others argue that coral reefs contain a greater variety of species. There is no way of proving who is right. But if we want to maintain biodiversity, we need to protect both rainforests and reefs.

How to wreck a reef

Reefs need sunlight and clean water to survive. Harmful local activities might include destroying parts of the reef, perhaps to build a marina or an airstrip, or building coastal roads, which produces debris that is washed into the sea, where it smothers the coral. Felling forests, even far inland, can make rivers run thick with silt as the forest soil is eroded. When the silt flows into the sea, it makes life impossible for coral. All these problems can be avoided by careful local planning.

Remote causes of reef damage are much harder to control. They may be caused by distant oil-spills or other forms of marine pollution, or by something much longer-term.

In the 1980s scientists began to notice the spread of coral 'bleaching', which means, as its name suggests, reefs turning white. This happens when the tiny plant cells that live within the coral and provide its food lose their photosynthetic pigments. It is caused by a rise in temperature, the result of the gradual change of climate usually known as global warming.

The temperature rise does not have to be very big to cause damage. A long hot summer, with water temperatures only 1 or 2 degrees Celsius above normal, can cause bleaching, though the coral will recover when cooler weather returns. However, even a few days of temperatures 4 degrees above normal will cause bleaching from which only 5 or 10 per cent of coral will recover. Politicians and environmentalists all over the world are trying to find a cure for global warming, so far without success.

VIEWPOINT

'We are currently witnessing the extinction of all offshore corals in the western Atlantic and we are also seeing the start of this development in the Indo-Pacific. If we do not react immediately and rigorously ... there will be no future for offshore coral reefs.'
Arnfried Antonius, Institute of Palaeontology, Vienna University, 2000

Bleached staghorn coral on the Great Barrier Reef, Australia.

FACT

Scientists estimate that 10 per cent of the world's coral reefs have been lost in the last fifty years, with 30 per cent in immediate danger and another 30 per cent that could be lost by 2050. Nobody knows how many animal species would be wiped out if this happened.

Glorious mud

Our ancestors who lived among the vast bogs and fenlands that covered large parts of Europe and North America regarded them as dangerous places, to be avoided where possible. They sacrificed people to the spirits of these awesome places, as we know from finding human remains in places in Denmark, like Schleswig, where a young girl was drowned in shallow water, or Tollund, where a man was strangled with a leather thong, both about two thousand years ago. When humans eventually developed the technology they needed to drain the fens (around AD 1000) they must have leapt at the chance.

The soil that emerged was rich and fertile, full of nutrients, unlike the poor soil left when a forest is felled. When it had dried out, it was ideal for building, being completely level. (Sometimes the building proved to be a mistake, as at Mexico City, built on a drained lake-bottom which is liable to subsidence causing earthquakes – but that was centuries after the site was chosen.) Land 'reclaimed' from fenland and seashore seemed like a gift.

'Unproductive' wetlands, like the Volga Delta in Russia, may be useless to humans, but they are vital to an enormous range of other life forms.

One small bog near Marseilles, France, contains breeding populations of no less than twelve species of large dragonfly. Many of them are found nowhere else for miles around, because all nearby wetlands have been drained.

The marsh fritillary butterfly has disappeared from much of Europe.

'...the accelerating rates of warming we can expect in the coming decades are likely to put large numbers of species at risk. Climate change may lead to the disappearance or transformation of extensive areas of important wildlife habitat – many species will be unable to move fast enough to survive.'
World Wide Fund for Nature web site, 2000

'Is global warming a real problem, or just another phony eco-scare?'
Steven Milloy, biostatistician and lawyer, attached to the Cato Institute, USA, 2000

One man's gift...

But the gift to humanity was theft from other living creatures. Wetlands of all kinds, including bogs and marshes, river estuaries and shallow lakes, teem with life, from dragonflies and waterlilies to frogs and fish. They are also vital staging posts for millions of migrating wildfowl and other water birds as they move from their summer breeding grounds to the warmer places where they spend the winter.

Furthermore, they play an important part in maintaining the earth's nitrogen balance. Bacteria that are abundant in wetlands break down nitrates and nitrites to release the free nitrogen that forms four-fifths of our atmosphere.

FACT

The whooping crane in North America is a conservation success story. In the 1940s there were only about twenty survivors, but careful protection of their breeding and wintering places led to their recovery. By 1996 there were 205 adults in the wild, including a single flock of 165 birds.

Nitrogen has been described as the earth's 'fire blanket'. Without it, the atmosphere would be so rich in oxygen that the whole planet would have burned to a cinder millions of years ago.

Yet wetlands are being drained at an increasing rate, and only a tiny percentage of them have been left unharmed. Endangered long-distance migrants, like the whooping crane in North America and its cousin the European crane, have to fly further and further between their traditional resting and feeding places as the years go by. The European crane breeds from Scandinavia and Germany through to Russia, and winters in north-west and east Africa, so it needs plenty of 'service stations' on the way.

Sandhill cranes are still abundant in North America, their haunting cries acting as a bugle-call for wetland conservation.

Money and motives

It is not easy to persuade people in general that places need to be saved for their own sake. A stretch of upland bog, even if it is one of the last in Europe, an unkempt piece of woodland, or a featureless patch of the Nevada desert, are not of obvious value to everyone.

The word 'wilderness', often used by conservationists as if it were reason enough on its own for spending money to preserve some far corner of the earth, has a different meaning for the general public. The dictionary equates it with 'desolate', 'wild' and other negative qualities. Images of the wolf-infested wild wood and the spirit-haunted swamp are still strong in the collective consciousness.

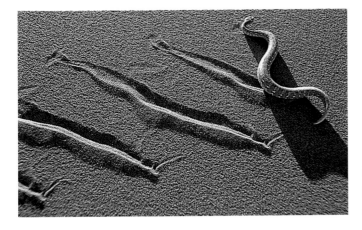

Can a poisonous sidewinder adder, rather less cuddly than a panda, act as ambassador for the world's deserts?

Because of this, the publicity campaigns to raise money to save such places need a different focus. This is why, in their efforts to save habitat, fund-raisers often concentrate on the species that live there. We are invited to help save not a bog or a wood but a dragonfly or a pretty little bird. Not a desert but a – what? Rattlesnake? Hunting spider? Or perhaps a mountain lion? Maybe that is far enough from most people's experience not to be too frightening.

Because not everyone understands the need to protect the remaining wild habitats in the world, the ways of persuading the public must be very carefully thought out if we are to succeed in leaving a wild world for the benefit of our descendants – and of the plants and animals with which we share our planet.

Wars over whales

In the 1960s, whaling was a reputable, even glamorous business, carried out by heroic mariners in some of the world's wildest waters. At that time, some 60,000 whales were being killed every year. By the early 1970s everything had changed: whaling was widely regarded as immoral, cruel, and economically unjustified by all but a handful of nations. In 1972 the United Nations held a Conference on the Human Environment in Stockholm, at which fifty-two countries voted for an immediate end to commercial whaling. No-one voted for it to continue.

All the same, the hunt went on, carried out by Russia, Iceland, Japan, Norway and Australia. In 1977, a campaign called Project Jonah won an independent inquiry into whaling policy. In 1978 Australia banned whaling, and became the first nation to state that whaling was morally wrong. That left Norway, Russia and Japan as the only nations still killing whales commercially. Iceland said it had given up but it was still involved, as we shall see.

Gory glory days: nineteenth-century whalers were almost insanely brave in pursuit of their valuable prey.

To kill a humpback whale would be unthinkable today, but they may have passed the point of no return.

VIEWPOINTS

'The Japanese are already killing up to 500 minke whales a year … for "scientific" purposes. It is my belief that this data will be used to … justify a request for resumption of legitimate commercial whaling.'
Per Madie, Director, Cetacean Investigation Centre

'Current estimates place the North Pacific minke population at a robust 25,000, but despite [scientific] findings … that this population could easily sustain a harvest of 200+ whales a year, the IWC continues to impose a zero quota on the Japanese [whale] harvest.'
Japanese page of World Council of Whalers website, 2000

Japan claims that its whaling tradition 'stretches back unbroken over millennia' and Norway says that it has been whaling 'for several thousand years'.

Both countries use the meat that they kill exclusively for home consumption: in Japan it sells for high prices in special whale-meat restaurants. However, Japan also buys whale meat from Iceland, the product of what is described as 'scientific' whaling. This is supposed to study whale populations by marking and releasing individuals: in effect, though, it kills whales worth tens of millions of dollars for the Japanese market.

Eight out of the ten species of great whale are now considered 'commercially extinct' (that is, not worth the effort of hunting because they are too hard to find). They are: right, bowhead, gray, blue, humpback, fin, sei and Bryde's whales. Sperm whales and bottlenosed or beaked whales still exist in reasonable numbers. The gray whale is the only species to recover from intensive whaling: after being protected for decades, the blue, bowhead and humpback have not increased their numbers. When animals range over such a huge area, their population can fall so low that not enough whales meet to breed. These whales are on the road to extinction.

THE WAY AHEAD

CITES, IUCN, WWF, FFI, SCMU – no, it's not a coded message, but a list of some of the many international conservation bodies operating today.

Smuggling ivory is big business. Here, French customs officers inspect 628 smuggled ivory carvings intercepted in Paris in 1999, on their way from Rwanda to Japan.

CITES is the Convention on the International Trade in Endangered Species of Wild Fauna and Flora. This was signed by 125 countries in Washington DC in 1973, and came into force in 1975. Other nations have signed it since, and in July 2000 there were 152 signatories. However, as we have seen, although international trade is important in the conservation of some species (especially rhinos and tigers), it is not the main threat to all wildlife today. Loss of habitat is much more important.

Some people say that, by limiting the trade in wild animals, and therefore the benefits that people can get from them, CITES has made it less worthwhile for local people to protect the wildlife habitat around them. The human (and preferably humane) use of wildlife might actually be an incentive to conservation. People who were earning money from wild animals would make sure that they did not wipe out the valuable stock. Trade is opposed by people who think that to make any use of wildlife is wrong: but if it could be controlled, trade might be the best way ahead.

Strong advocates of resuming trade in wild animals come from southern countries, especially in Africa, whereas the Convention was drawn up by conservationists from the northern hemisphere, who have a different view of the problem. We have seen how three southern African countries managed to gain a concession from CITES over the matter of selling their ivory. Just how legitimate ivory can be identified is one question. Whether the renewed trade will stimulate the market and encourage further poaching is another.

IUCN is the International Union for the Conservation of Nature, a body whose main duty is to monitor and report conservation activities, especially through the Species Survival Commission (SSC). WWF is the World Wide Fund for Nature, which raises funds to be used in conservation work. FFI is Flora and Fauna International, another fund-raising body which also co-ordinates research all over the world, publishing the results in the important journal *Oryx*. SCMU is the Species Conservation Monitoring Unit, based in Cambridge, England. This is a more academic concern, but with the same aims as the IUCN and SSC. And that's enough alphabet soup for now.

FACT

Recent research by biological investigator Esmond Martin in Egypt, where more illegal ivory is sold than anywhere else in Africa, shows that most of it comes from elephants poached in Central and West Africa. Egypt is a member of CITES, but does not enforce its 1990 ban on international trade in ivory.

DEBATE

Has CITES served its purpose? What should it be doing now?

Small is beautiful

Smaller organizations, such as national, state, county or town bird clubs and botanical societies, bring conservation closer to ordinary people, making them feel that they are doing something for their local environment.

Whether you see ducks as beautiful or delicious, protecting their habitat benefits many other species, as well as sportsmen.

For example, Ducks Unlimited is a national organization in the USA, divided into local branches. In one operation, its members have reclaimed the dried-up Sacramento Delta in California, returning it to wetlands by controlled flooding of cornfields that had long since turned into a dustbowl. In return for their efforts, they now attract plenty of ducks every winter, when they migrate southwards from their Canadian breeding grounds. Some are even breeding in the Delta, without bothering to migrate.

Conservation with a bang

The members of Ducks Unlimited gather at the new wetlands on crisp winter mornings, and shoot the ducks. This causes consternation among some environmentalists, but it is a perfect example of practical conservation.

The considerable cost of the work was borne by the members themselves, because they wanted better sport. The numbers they may shoot are determined after the breeding success of each species has been measured in the Fall. The result is a lot of happy shooters, and a very large number of contented ducks.

A project like this is a signpost for the way ahead, beginning to put right the sad state of affairs in the USA, which has lost more than half its original wetlands in the lower forty-eight states – mainly to agriculture (as in the Delta).

Another type of potentially scandalous conservation operation is found in Africa, where the use of wildlife by local people is taken to what some might say is an extreme. In South Africa, Namibia and Zimbabwe – and in some other countries too – landowners do a brisk business in organizing hunting safaris, playing host to wealthy sportsmen from overseas, mainly North America, Europe and Japan.

The visitors are guided out into the bush, and shown which animals they can shoot. Plainly the owner does not want them to kill all his game animals, so he selects those that can be spared from the stock, usually large old males, past their breeding peak. Since this is exactly what the sportsmen want, to take home to decorate their dens, both sides are happy.

VIEWPOINT

'If Zambia put together a hunting package in the Luangwa Valley, which permitted a foreign hunter to kill one rhino bull, two elephant bulls and two buffalo bulls ... it would generate foreign currency in excess of $30,000 (US) for each hunt offered. This would make wildlife more valuable to the rural black people than any single thing in their lives.'
Ron Thomson, Director, Bophuthatswana National Parks.

A proud hunter with his quarry, a Burchell's zebra.

The S word

Sustainability is the key to conservation in the twenty-first century. It means not taking from any resource more than it can replace naturally. Whaling is a clear example of an unsustainable 'harvest', in which animals were killed as fast as technology would allow, without any thought for how quickly they were breeding. Some people compare it with mining or oil-drilling.

A 1000 tonne catch of tuna being landed in New South Wales. Can fishing at this intensity be sustainable?

Most modern fisheries still use the same approach, in spite of strong evidence that stocks are dwindling all over the world. Recent research shows that the tuna is on the brink of becoming an endangered species, because too many fish are being taken without any regard as to how quickly the population can recover. In October 1996, the southern bluefin tuna was added to the IUCN Red List of Endangered Species.

A farmer who breeds cattle for the market must run a sustainable operation if he is to stay in business, killing and selling only those animals that can be replaced by his breeding herd. Similarly, an African tribe that wants to profit from the sale of ivory must take care not to kill more elephants than the population can replace. Some would argue that we should not make use of ivory at all, but use plastics instead: but this is to ignore the large amount of money that can be made from ivory by countries that might not have many other resources.

At a less controversial level, killing game for meat can also be done in a sustainable way. As long ago as 1961, Julian Huxley wrote a report for UNESCO in which he pointed out that organized hunting in Africa would work to the advantage of wild animal populations, by making sure that populations remain viable. The organized shooting of ducks on the Sacramento Delta is a case in point.

Is Africa a zoo?

Huxley also wrote about the likely importance of tourism as a way for local people to benefit from living alongside spectacular wild animals. At that time, long-distance air travel was an expensive luxury. But now many people travel thousands of miles for their holidays. For a number of African countries, especially, tourism is an important source of income from abroad, and what the tourists come to see is the animals.

Just like on TV: a photographic safari in Kenya's Masai Mara National Park.

VIEWPOINTS

'Each area needs its own special agreements and measures to protect the stocks. The EU dictating solutions to fishermen from afar is resented and has not worked. I still think it can be done, stock can recover, there is still all to play for.'
Barry Dees, Chief Executive of the National Federation of Fishermen's Organisations

'Unless we take action to regenerate fish stocks, jobs in the fishing industry and the future of coastal communities will continue to suffer decline... We're not asking people to stop fishing or eating fish. Fishermen and WWF share the same goal – abundant fish stocks in healthy seas.'
Alastair Davison, World Wide Fund for Nature, Scotland

FACT

The orang-utan once lived all over Indochina, and from Malaysia up to China. It now lives only on Sumatra and Borneo. Its decline was due to hunting for pets, which has now been banned, malaria, and loss of habitat. There are still about 20,000 orangutans but, even now, their rainforest habitat is being felled around them.

A young orang-utan in Tanjung Puting National Park, Borneo.

VIEWPOINTS

'The global exinction crisis is as bad as or worse than believed, with dramatic declines of many species, including reptiles and primates.'
IUCN Red List of Endangered Species 2000

'The beauty of working in conservation is you see the ability of nature to bounce back. History is littered with examples of mammals reduced to tens of individuals making a comeback.'
Stuart Chapman, World Wide Fund for Nature, UK

To a country like Zambia, for example, a healthy population of elephants and rhino is just as valuable as the Mayan temples of Central America or the beaches of the Costa del Sol, as a way of attracting tourists. However, there are objections to this from two points of view.

Some conservationists, Africans among them, regret that Africa seems destined to become little more than a huge zoo, where people go to gape at the animals. Many Africans also resent the idea that their countries' only way ahead is to stand still, not to become modern industrial economies. Must they abandon progress just so that people from abroad can come and marvel at wildlife that they cannot see at home, because their ancestors wiped it out centuries ago?

Their visitors then go home to their motorways and air-conditioned shopping malls, leaving Africa stuck in the nineteenth century. The same applies to other countries where the survival of endangered species depends on maintaining wild habitat at the expense of the people who live there. This is one of the rockier parts of the road ahead, and at present there is no clear map to show the best way to go.

This land is our land

However, there are some pointers. The key may be to develop a link between local people and protected areas. For instance, the local people could gain some benefit from the reserve, perhaps by earning money from tourists. Or they could be allowed to harvest the resources, within sustainable limits. Finally, the reserve could be handed over to the local community to manage for themselves. This seems to be the fairest way. But it is also perhaps the riskiest, as it relies on the local people being persuaded that maintaining biodiversity is as important as making a living.

· *Hope for the future: schoolchildren in Rome demonstrate at an international global warming conference, carrying placards showing animals endangered by climate change.*

It is not going to be easy. But the alternative is to accept that the wild places of the world will gradually vanish, and the endangered species with them. If that happens there will be only one endangered species left on the planet: our own.

GLOSSARY

aphrodisiac a medicine or charm that is supposed to improve a person's sex life.

arable land used for growing crops.

arachnophobia uncontrollable fear of spiders.

autonomous self-governing.

biodiversity variety of forms of life.

bivouac temporary shelter, crude tent.

carrying capacity the number of animals of a particular species that an area can support.

clearance cutting down trees in order to clear land for farming.

dilemma a problem with two conflicting answers.

fallow land that is left uncultivated.

feral (an animal) once tame or domesticated, living in the wild.

forager someone who is looking for food.

genetic diversity a variety of different adult animals to breed from.

hunter-gatherers people who live by hunting animals and gathering plant food.

indigenous native to a region.

lucrative very profitable; enabling someone to earn a great deal of money.

marsupial a mammal that raises its young in a pouch, like a kangaroo.

midden a dump where bones and other rubbish are left.

migratory travelling from one place to another as the seasons change.

millinery trade making and decorating hats.

nomadic wandering, with no fixed home.

palaeontologist a person who studies fossils.

pastoralist a person who keeps herds of grazing animals.

phobia an uncontrollable fear.

photosynthetic pigments that plants use to make food from sunlight. The most common is chlorophyll, which makes leaves green.

primate member of the group of animals that includes apes, monkeys and humans.

quadruped animal with four legs.

stock the number of animals available to catch.

sub-fossil old remains that are not yet fossilized (turned to stone).

subsistence farming growing food and raising animals to eat, not to sell.

trophies stuffed and mounted heads of horned animals.

tundra open grassland that is frozen for most of the year.

viable able to survive.

wetlands collective term for rivers, lakes, marshes, etc.

BOOKS TO READ

The Atlas of Endangered Species, 2nd edition
John A. Burton (ed)
(Macmillan, USA, 1999)

Cod: A Biography of the Fish that Changed the World
Mark Kurlansky
(Jonathan Cape, 1998)
History of the destruction of the cod fishery

The End of Nature
Bill McKibben
(Viking, 1990)
Vanishing wilderness

Endangered Sealife
World Conservation Monitoring Centre
(World Book International, USA, 1995)

Foxes, Wolves and Wild Dogs of the World,
2nd edition
D. Alderton
(Cassell Illustrated, 1998)

The Gardeners of Eden
Alistair Graham
(George Allen & Unwin, 1973)
Criticism of conservation methods

International Wildlife Trade: Whose Business is It?
Sarah Fitzgerald
(WWF, 1989)

Pandas
Chris Catton
(Christopher Helm, 1990)

Saving All the Parts
Rocky Barker
(Island Press, 1993)
Living in a sensitive ecosystem, US Pacific North-west

The Song of the Dodo
David Quammen
(Hutchinson, 1996)
Extinction worldwide

Threatened Birds of the World
A.J. Stattersfield and D.R. Capper (eds)
(Birdlife International, Cambridge, 2000)

The Whale War
David Day
(Routledge & Kegan Paul, 1987)

Wild Cats of the World
D. Alderton
(Facts on File Inc. 2003)

Wolf Wars
Hank Fischer
(Falcon Press, 1995)

USEFUL
ADDRESSES

www.panda.org
World Wide Fund for Nature.

http://www.wwf-uk.org/
The UK site for the World Wide Fund
for Nature.

http://www.greenpeace.org
Greenpeace.

http://www.foe.org
The US site for Friends of the Earth.

http://www.foe.org.uk
The UK site for Friends of the Earth.

http://www.iucn.org
IUCN, the World's Conservation Union.

http://www.redlist.org
The IUCN Red List of Endangered Species.

http://www.wcs.org
Wildlife Conservation Society.

http://www.bornfree.org.uk/
The Born Free Foundation – an animal
welfare and conservation charity dedicated to
conserving endangered species and protecting
wildlife habitats.

http://www.globaltigerpatrol.co.uk
Global Tiger Patrol – a conservation agency
mainly focusing on protection of the tiger in
the wild.

http://www.worldcouncilofwhalers.com
The World Council of Whalers –
a pro-whaling site.

http://csiwhalesalive.org/
The Cetacean Society International –
an anti-whaling site.

Friends of the Earth
26-28 Underwood Street
London N1 7JQ
Tel: 0207 490 1555

Greenpeace
Canonbury Villas
London N1 2PN
Tel: 0207 865 8100

World Wide Fund for Nature – International
Avenue du Mont-Blanc
CCH-1196
Gland
Switzerland
Tel: +41 22 364 9111

**World Wide Fund for Nature – United
Kingdom**
Panda House
Weyside Park
Godalming
Surrey GU7 1XR
Tel: +44 1483 426 444

INDEX